Hi Readers!

It can be scary trying something new, right? Jumping off a diving board for the first time. Eating a different food. Going to a new school. Making a friend. New and different things can feel scary, but they can also become exciting adventures.

We chose Mae Jemison to be the feature of our second issue because she never let her fears stop her from accomplishing her goals. It was curiosity, not fear, that drove her to do great things. Even though Mae was afraid of the dark, she traveled into the darkness of the universe. Though Mae was afraid of heights, she orbited hundreds of miles above the earth. Despite her fears, Mae boarded a space shuttle and rocketed into the deep, dark unknown.

Being brave even when it's scary is hard. Guess what? This issue of *Bravery* was scary for us. In this issue, we talk about fear, but we also talk about things that we don't have much experience with. The two of us have never had to go through what Mae Jemison and other people of color go through every day. What we have learned through this process is that there is so much to learn! We stepped into the unknown of how to have conversations about differences and discovered incredible things when we did. Space was Mae Jemison's uncharted territory. This issue is our uncharted territory.

Ashley at age 7

Elyse at age 7

We hope that the story of Mae Jemison will inspire you as much as it has us—that it will create opportunities to have more conversations with each other about important things like race, equity, and representation. We hope that the real, brave women you read about in *Bravery Magazine* will inspire you to step into the unknown and be your own kind of brave.

ASHLEY + ELYSE

STORIES + ESSAYS

ACTIVITIES

Submitted by Michelle Sneider

TABLE OF CONTENTS

DREAMING

LEARNING

DOING

YOU

HEADS UP
We have a section in the back just for parents. Any title in orange can be found there.

"Never limit yourself because of others' limited imaginations; never limit others because of your limited imagination."

MAE JEMISON

Born in Alabama, USA on October 17, 1956

YOUNG MAE

A star is born

Illustrations by Maggie Cole

When Mae was five years old, her kindergarten teacher asked her class what they wanted to be when they grew up. Mae stood up proudly and said, "I want to be a scientist!" Her teacher asked, "Don't you mean a nurse?" This bothered Mae. Unfortunately, many people, especially during that time, didn't think women or people of color could be scientists.

Confidently, Mae put her hands on her hips and said, "No, I mean a scientist." Mae knew exactly what she wanted to become. Her parents had taught her that she could be anything she wanted to be, no matter what other people thought.

Mae continued to learn and grew more confident as she got older. She loved to follow her older brother and sister around and try to be like them.

Often, they played tricks on her. Sometimes they even shut her in the dark basement. Mae was afraid of the dark, but she tried not to let her fear stop her from doing things she wanted to do.

Mae loved dancing and wanted to take dance classes. Her mother said she could, but the class was far away, so Mae had to take an elevated train all by herself to get there. The "el" train was high off the ground. Mae was afraid of heights, but she wanted to dance so badly that she taught herself to be brave.

Mae climbed the stairs onto the high platform and tried not to look down; the ground was so far away! She stepped onto the train, carefully climbed down the steps at her stop, then walked to her dance class. Mae controlled her fear long enough to accomplish something she wanted to do. She learned to dance!

Mae loved to learn and she always asked questions. She often walked to the public library and read books about stars, planets, and the universe.

Some of her favorite books were science fiction novels — stories about people living in space. She always imagined herself solving space mysteries and going on dangerous missions to help save the earth.

Mae often stayed at the library all day and walked home at night when it closed. She loved to look up into the sky and see the stars twinkling overhead. Mae imagined herself working at an observatory and wondered if the same stars were in the sky when dinosaurs lived on Earth.

Because Mae and her family were African American, she was taught to be proud of who she was, even if many people said and thought mean things about her because of her race.

Mae's parents taught her to love and accept others even if they were different or unkind.

While Mae was young, a civil rights movement was taking place in America. African Americans were not allowed basic rights in the United States because they were black.

Dr. Martin Luther King, Jr. was a great man who was one of the leaders of the civil rights movement. He fought for equality for African Americans, but he was killed for his beliefs

when Mae was 10. People around the country showed their anger and pain through civil demonstrations, and sometimes it wasn't safe to go outside, so Mae's family stayed inside their house.

One day, Mae looked out her window and saw soldiers marching past her home. She felt scared, angry, and confused. Sitting at the window, Mae made herself a promise that she would not let other people make her be afraid again. She would do the things she knew were right and she would help people. She would not hurt others or scare them.

It was around this time that Mae knew she would go to space no matter what. She loved to watch spaceships take off and followed the NASA space program.

At the time, only white men were allowed to go to space. There were no women astronauts and Mae didn't like that. Mae loved a challenge, so she set her sights on becoming an astronaut even when everyone said she couldn't do it.

Mae loved learning and worked very hard. She went to high school when she was only 12 years old. Mae was very creative and liked to try lots of new things.

She did research projects, learned different languages, acted in plays, performed in dances, and she even designed and made clothes for dolls, but Mae loved science most of all. She graduated from high school at 16 and earned a scholarship to study science at Stanford University in California.

DID YOU KNOW MAE WAS AFRAID OF THE DARK WHEN SHE WAS LITTLE?

what are you afraid of?

Fear is only a weakness if it stops you from being curious. Mae didn't let her fear of darkness stop her from going to space.

SEEING STARS

Constellations are groupings of stars in the sky. Thousands of years ago, scientists thought these groups of stars looked like shapes, so they gave the constellations names that described them. Look up and you might see lions, dragons, kings, and fish in the sky.

URSA MINOR
the lesser bear

CASSIOPEIA
the Queen

CANCER
the crab

CRUX
southern cross

CAPRICORNUS
the sea goat

PISCES
the fishes

WANT TO SEE CONSTELLATIONS WITHOUT LEAVING YOUR HOUSE?

Use a pin to poke holes in the stars of the constellations above. Find a dark room, hold your paper up near a blank wall, and shine a flashlight at your paper. What do you see?

HOW TO BE A SCIENTIST
CURIOSITY IS KEY!

Scientists are curious -- they ask questions and find creative ways to solve problems. They use a process called the scientific method to help find answers to their questions. Below, you'll find a silly example of the scientific method in action.

1. MAKE AN OBSERVATION...

2. ASK A QUESTION

3. MAKE A HYPOTHESIS OR A GUESS

4. CONDUCT YOUR EXPERIMENT

5. DRAW YOUR CONCLUSIONS

...WHAT DID YOU LEARN?

6. RECORD/REPORT your RESULTS

WHAT'S THE SCIENTIFIC METHOD? TURN TO PAGE 13 TO FIND OUT

GUMMY BEAR EXPERIMENT

A hands-on activity using the Scientific Method

SUPPLIES:

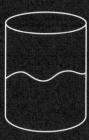

Water

Small Bowls or Containers

Other Liquids such as Milk, Vinegar, Soda etc.

Baking Soda

Salt

Small Bag of Gummy Bears

instructions up ahead

THE SCIENTIFIC METHOD IN ACTION

Write some observations about your gummy bears. What color are they, what do they smell like, etc.

What do you think will happen to your gummy bears when you put them in different liquids? Write your hypothesis below.

Conduct your experiment!

What did you learn from your experiment? Was your hypothesis right? Did the gummy bears get bigger, smaller, or stay the same size? Record your results below.

LIQUID	BIGGER	SMALLER	STAYED THE SAME
water			

LET'S GET STARTED

STEP 1

In a small bowl, mix one teaspoon of salt into 1/3 cup of warm water until the salt dissolves. In another small bowl, mix one teaspoon of baking soda into 1/3 cup of water until it dissolves.

STEP 2

Fill the rest of your bowls with the other liquids you've chosen to use (1/3 cup each). Sort through your gummy bears and pick ones that look to be about the same size. For each liquid, choose two gummy bears that are the same color.

STEP 3

Place one gummy bear in each liquid and a matching colored gummy bear next to the corresponding bowl. This will help you be able to watch the changes and compare each gummy bear in liquid to a normal gummy bear. Let your gummy bears sit in their liquids for 3-6 hours. Watch the changes and record your results afterwards.

MOONWALK

Gravity-free Gliding

Mae loved to dance. She started dancing when she was a little girl and hasn't stopped since. The Moonwalk is a special dance move that makes you look like you're gliding on the surface of the moon. It works best on a smooth surface and with cool socks on your feet.

1. Start with your feet together facing forward
2. Bend your right foot in tiptoe position next to the heel of your left foot
3. Put all of your weight on your right foot and slide your left foot backwards
4. Pop your left foot into tiptoe position next to your right heel and push your right heel down so your foot is flat.
5. Now slide your right foot back into tiptoe position by your left heel and push your left heel down so your foot is flat. You should be moving backwards.
6. Repeat the steps and keep practicing. You'll be gliding before you know it!

MAE AT SCHOOL
Shooting for the moon

Illustrations by Maggie Cole

Mae moved to California all by herself and started studying. She wanted to be a scientist and help other people. Because she was young, a girl, and African American, the teachers at her college would not listen to Mae. They ignored her when she asked questions, so she worked extra hard to prove that she belonged.

Mae had been taught that she was important and to believe in herself, so she knew she could do hard things and accomplish her dreams.

When Mae was 20, she went to medical school at Cornell University. She worked very hard and learned all about the human body. During the summer, Mae traveled to many different countries to help other people.

She helped with surgeries and gave people medicine who didn't have any. Mae traveled to Thailand, Cuba, and several countries in Africa to help bring medicine to the people who lived there. When Mae was done with school, she became a doctor, but never forgot her dream of going to space.

MAE AROUND THE

Chicago

Mae grew up in Chicago. She was curious and loved science and the stars.

Stanford (CA)

She graduated from high school at 16 and went to Stanford University. Mae studied chemical engineering as well as African and Afro-American studies.

Cornell (NY)

Mae traveled to New York to go to medical school. She became a doctor at age 24.

Kenya

During medical school, Mae traveled to Africa to help the people there who didn't have access to doctors or medicine.

WORLD

She's going places!

Thailand

In Thailand, Mae worked at a Cambodian refugee camp, treating patients and helping refugees feel better.

Sierra Leone

After medical school, Mae joined the Peace Corps and became a medical officer. She provided medical care for the doctors there.

Cuba

Mae also helped sick people in Cuba. She knew everyone deserved basic medical care, so she worked hard to provide it for others.

Liberia

Mae was also a Peace Corps medical officer in Liberia. While there, she taught other doctors and did research.

Next stop: SPACE

MAE GOES TO SPACE

Three, two, one...blast off!

Illustrations by Maggie Cole

Without telling anybody, Mae applied to NASA's space program. One day while Mae was helping a patient at her health clinic, NASA headquarters called to give her the good news. Mae's dream was coming true — she was going to space! There were 2,000 people who wanted to become astronauts, and Mae was one out of only 15 people chosen.

Astronauts have to be healthy, strong, and able to learn new skills, so Mae had to practice learning new things to become a real astronaut. In space, there is very little gravity, so astronauts float around. Mae had to learn how it felt to be weightless. It made her really sick.

Mae also had to learn how to survive if their spaceship crashed or landed in the wrong place. She learned how to build fires, make a shelter, and find water.

Mae worked very hard to become an astronaut, and on September 12, 1992, Mae became the first woman of color in the WORLD to fly to space!

As the spaceship Endeavor rocketed away from earth and into space, Mae was excited that the first thing she saw out the window was Chicago, the place where she grew up.

Mae had a special job in space. She was a Science Mission Specialist — she got to do experiments in space. Mae conducted experiments to figure out why people get sick when they go to space and tried to find ways to help them feel better. She also did experiments on tadpoles!

Mae tried to celebrate art and creativity in space, so she brought some special things with her. She wanted to include people who didn't have the opportunity to fly to space like she did. She brought a poster of her favorite African American dancer, a special flag, and a statue made by women in West Africa.

Mae was in space for eight days and orbited the earth 127 times. Mae wasn't afraid in space. As her space shuttle prepared to come back to Earth, Mae looked out the window at the stars. She remembered how much she loved space when she was a little girl and it made her smile. If little Mae could see her now! Mae always knew she'd be in space and she felt right at home. Mae was happy and knew she was right where she belonged.

FOR THE REST OF MAE'S STORY, TURN TO PAGE 38

MAE WAS ONE OF 15 PEOPLE CHOSEN TO GO TO SPACE OUT OF OVER 2,000 APPLICANTS. CAN YOU FIND HER? HINT: SHE HAS EARRINGS

SPACE IS FOR EVERYONE

When Mae Jemison went to space, she took special items with her that represented who she was. She also wanted to represent people on earth who might be left out or wouldn't have a chance to go to space. Below are pictures of what Mae brought to space with her.

A POSTER OF JUDITH JAMESON PERFORMING THE DANCE *CRY*

Cry is a ballet dance that was choreographed by Alvin Ailey for his mother. It is about women overcoming hard things and being strong. Judith Jameson performed it beautifully.

BUNDU STATUE

Mae was given a wooden bundu statue by a society of women from Sierra Leone in West Africa.

A FLAG

Mae took a banner for the Alpha Kappa Alpha sorority. Alpha Kappa Alpha is the oldest African American women's sorority in the United States.

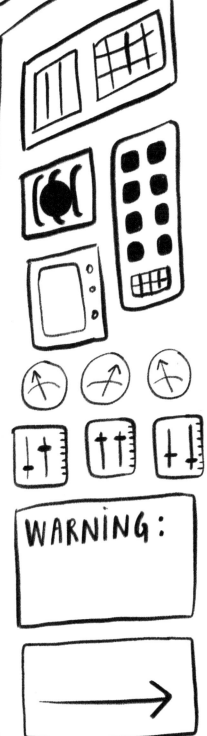

WHAT WOULD YOU BRING TO SPACE TO REPRESENT YOU?

DRAW HERE

WARNING:

Pluto

Neptune

Uranus

Venus

Earth

Mars

Mercury

Saturn

Jupiter

COLOR ME

SPACE "FIRSTS"

Astronauts that broke the mold and made history

1984
SVETLANA SAVITSKAYA
FIRST SPACE WALK
BY A WOMAN

1983
SALLY RIDE
FIRST AMERICAN
WOMAN & FIRST LGBT
PERSON IN SPACE

1992
MAE JEMISON
FIRST WOMAN OF
COLOR IN SPACE

1963
VALENTINA TERESHKOVA
FIRST WOMAN COSMONAUT

1969
NEIL ARMSTRONG
FIRST PERSON TO
WALK ON THE MOON

1961
YURI GAGARIN
FIRST HUMAN IN SPACE

MAKE YOUR OWN JETPACK

First stop, the moon. Next stop, Mars!

SUPPLIES:

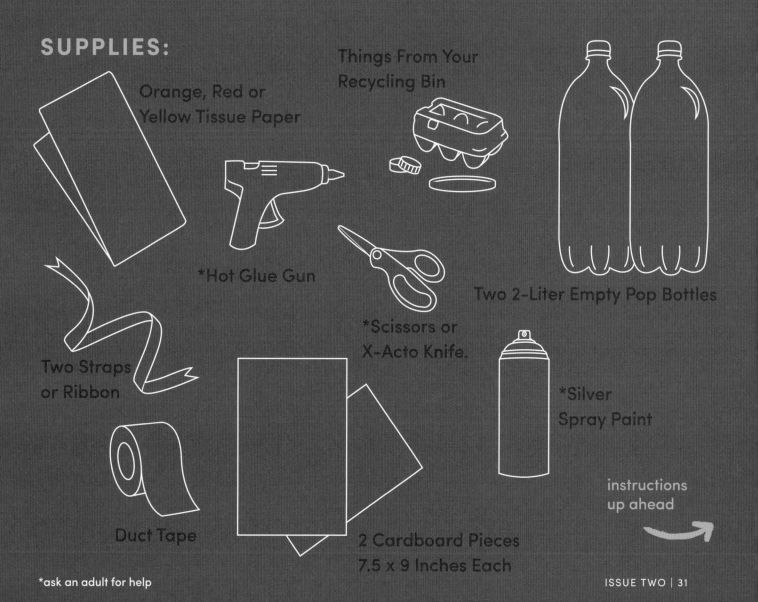

Orange, Red or Yellow Tissue Paper

Things From Your Recycling Bin

*Hot Glue Gun

*Scissors or X-Acto Knife.

Two 2-Liter Empty Pop Bottles

Two Straps or Ribbon

*Silver Spray Paint

Duct Tape

2 Cardboard Pieces 7.5 x 9 Inches Each

instructions up ahead

*ask an adult for help

LET'S GET STARTED

STEP 1

Empty two 2-liter pop bottles and tape them together with packing tape. Spray paint the bottles, cardboard, and extras you want to use on your jetpack (we used an egg carton and recycled lids). Let everything dry.

STEP 2

Ask an adult to use an X-Acto knife to cut four slits in the first cardboard square, one on each corner of the square. Thread your ribbon through these slits and tie together to create straps.

STEP 3

Assemble! Ask an adult to help you hot glue your supplies onto the remaining cardboard square to create a dashboard. Hot glue your dashboard piece onto one side of the pop bottles. Hot glue your straps onto the opposite side of your pop bottles. Cut strips of tissue paper and twist the ends together to create "fire." Glue the ends onto the inside of the pop bottle mouth.

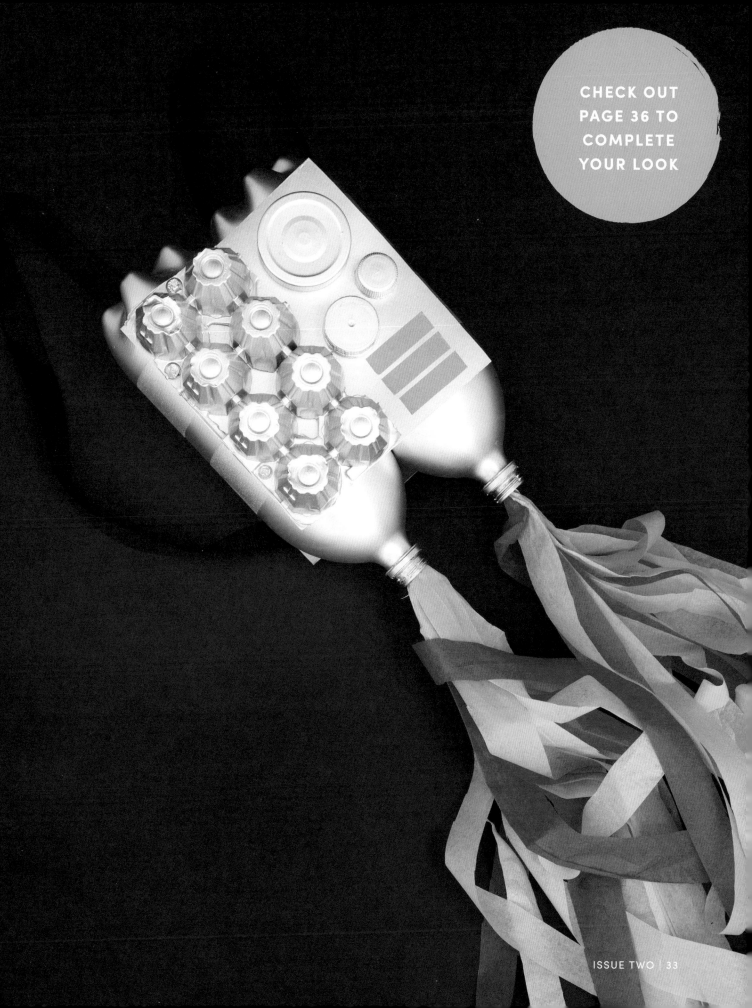

CHECK OUT
PAGE 36 TO
COMPLETE
YOUR LOOK

ASTRONAUT IN THE MAKING

Astronauts train for a long time to go to space. They exercise, study science, fix things underwater, and learn survival skills so they are ready for anything that space might throw at them. Complete your space training below to become an honorary astronaut.

Balance

Catch and throw a ball while balancing on one foot.

Dexterity

Do a puzzle with winter gloves on.

STRENGTH

Develop strong muscles.
Do 5–10 pushups and
5–10 squats.

ENDURANCE

Do 20 jumping jacks.

SURVIVAL

Build a fort using only
what's in the room.

FUELING STATION

Drink water and eat a
healthy snack.

HOW TO DRESS LIKE AN ASTRONAUT

You'll look out of this world

MAKE YOUR OWN
JETPACK ON
PAGE 31

MAKE YOUR OWN
HELMET OUT
OF PAPER
MACHE

SPRAY PAINT OLD
RAIN BOOTS FOR
THE PERFECT
MOON BOOT

SPRAY PAINT
OVEN MITTS
FOR SPACE
GLOVES

MAE MOVES ON
To infinity and beyond

Dr. Jemison at her health clinic.

A few years after her first space flight, Mae decided she didn't want to be an astronaut anymore. She wanted to find more ways that science and technology could help people all around the world, especially in developing countries. She created The Jemison Group, which helps research new ways technology can help make lives easier.

After she was an astronaut, Mae became a professor, wrote books, and starred on her favorite TV show, *Star Trek*. Mae still writes books for kids and speaks to large groups promoting science and technology.

Mae as a guest star on *Star Trek*.

Mae after starting the 100 Year Starship project.

Mae continues to ask hard questions and is a curious problem solver. She believes that as humans, we can all make a difference and become better. Mae is a changemaker and a role model. Her curiosity, hard work, and confidence inspires others to speak up and never give up on their dreams, no matter what someone else might say.

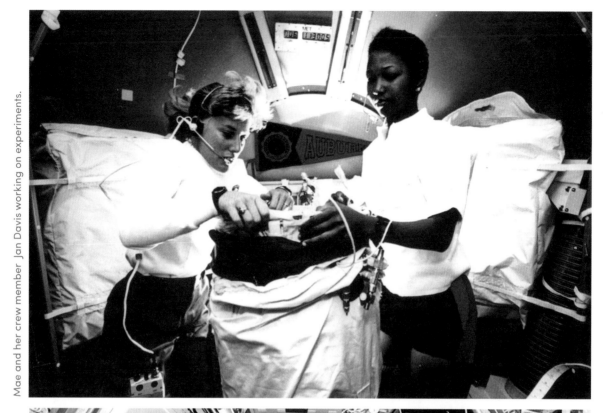

Mae and her crew member Jan Davis working on experiments.

Mae and her crew members aboard the Endeavor.

Mae believes it is very important for kids to learn about science in school, so she does everything she can to encourage all children regardless of race, gender, or circumstance to become interested in science and to speak up so they can change the world.

100 YEAR STARSHIP

Dr. Jemison has created a project that challenges humans to find ways to travel beyond our solar system in the next 100 years. Are you up for the challenge? Draw a starship below that can get humans to another solar system. Remember there are no grocery stores or fuel stations along the way so be sure and build a starship that could provide these resources.

JUPITER

VENUS

MERCURY

NEPTUNE

MOON

SATURN

EARTH

SUN

MARS

URANUS

PRO TIP:
HARD BOIL
YOUR EGGS FOR
LESS MESS

EGG DROP ROCKET SHIP

See if you can keep an egg from breaking when it's dropped from different heights

SUPPLIES:

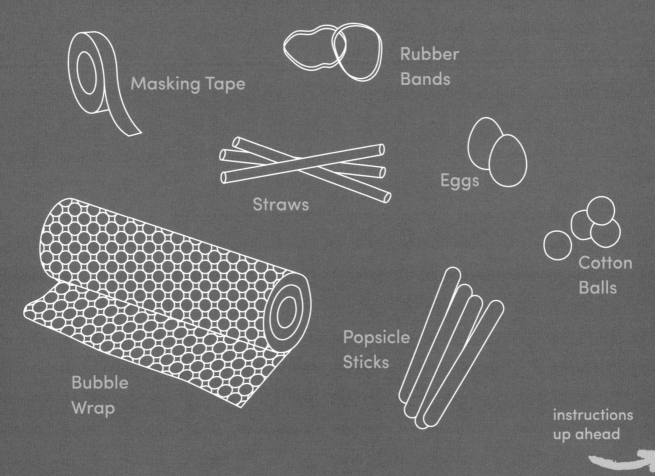

Masking Tape

Rubber Bands

Straws

Eggs

Cotton Balls

Bubble Wrap

Popsicle Sticks

instructions up ahead

*Use any supplies you have around your house. Above are some ideas.

DRAW AND DESCRIBE YOUR DESIGN PLAN

WHY DO YOU THINK YOUR DESIGN WILL PROTECT THE EGG?

_____

_____

_____

LET'S GET STARTED

STEP 1

Build your design. Use the supplies you gathered and your design plan on the previous page to build your spacecraft. Remember to protect your egg as much as you can so it won't crack when dropped.

STEP 2

Ask an adult for help and together find something high to stand on and drop your egg. Conduct an experiment to see what height you can drop your egg from without it breaking. If it didn't break, drop it from somewhere higher. If it did, go back to the drawing board. How can you protect your egg better?

STEP 3

Follow up. Did your design work? Why or why not? How could you improve your design? Record your findings.

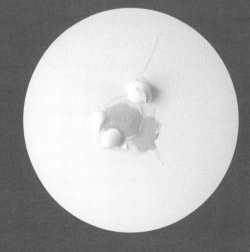

MAE'S UNIVERSE

Check out these fun facts about Mae and then answer the questions below. Maybe you'll find that you and Mae have something in common.

When Mae was younger, she couldn't decide if she wanted to be a dancer or a doctor. She loved both of them so much. Her mom told her, "You can always dance if you're a doctor, but you can't doctor if you're a dancer." Mae decided to become a doctor, but never stopped dancing.

Do you have two things

that you love to do?

Mae was inspired by Dr. Martin Luther King, Jr. She thought he was audacious and brave. Mae believed in Dr. King's dream of racial equality and thinks that "the best way to make dreams come true is to wake up."

Who is someone

you're inspired by?

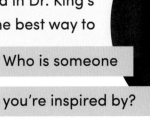

When she was growing up, Mae loved science fiction books. She enjoyed reading about characters who were brave and solved problems. She especially loved a book called *A Wrinkle in Time* by Madeleine L'Engle, because it featured women scientists and girl heroines in the story.

What is your favorite book?

MARTIAN MYSTERY

Can you crack this alien code? Use the symbols below to help you decipher the mysterious martian language.

NAME: Taylor
AGE: 14
FROM: Florida, US

EMAIL US AT
HELLO@BRAVERYMAG.COM
TO NOMINATE A
BRAVE KID

AAAAAVE KIDS

Look who's dreaming and doing

A LITTLE ABOUT TAYLOR:

Taylor Richardson is a voice of power. When she was nine, Taylor was inspired by Mae Jemison and became interested in space, so she raised funds to go to space camp. Later, Taylor was inspired by the movie *Hidden Figures*, so she raised over $20,000 to send 1,000 girls in her community to go see the movie. Taylor also started her own "Taylor's Take Flight with a Book" drive. She collects gently used books and donates them to local schools and neighborhoods. Currently she is raising funds to send young girls to see the movie *A Wrinkle in Time*. Taylor actively encourages girls to become involved in STEM and follow their dreams. She rises above stereotypes and judgments every day, always pushing towards her dream of becoming an astronaut and the first African American woman to go to Mars.

WHAT'S YOUR FAVORITE BOOK?

My first book that I read over and over that I really liked was *Bud, not Buddy* by Christopher Paul Curtis. And of course I love *Find Where the Wind Goes* by Mae Jemison.

WHAT IS YOUR FAVORITE FOOD?

Chicken tenders.

WHAT DO YOU LIKE TO DO FOR FUN?

Go to movies with friends and hang out at the mall.

WHAT IS YOUR FAVORITE SCHOOL SUBJECT?

Science.

WHO INSPIRES YOU?

Mae Jemison.

IF YOU COULD GO ANYWHERE IN SPACE, WHERE WOULD YOU GO?

Mars. It's unknown and unexplored.

WHAT DO YOU WANT TO DO ONCE YOU GET TO MARS?

Explore and collect items to help our planet.

WHAT INTERESTS YOU MOST ABOUT SPACE?

The stars and unknown. I want to know what is out there and if we can survive on other planets like Earth.

WOULD YOU RATHER GO TO SPACE FOR 5 MINUTES OR 5 YEARS?

Both. 5 minutes to say I did it, and then 5 years because I would want time to learn about the planet, explore and collect things that will hopefully make both planets a better place for us. But I would miss my family.

WHAT DOES BRAVERY MEAN TO YOU?

Owning my power. It's important to be the one who stands out in the crowd, who speaks up, and who must be a voice — either a voice people need to hear or a voice for others. Sometimes bravery means to pause, to sit in silence and to be okay with that too.

WHAT'S THE BRAVEST THING YOU'VE EVER DONE?

As a black girl, I'm brave by not conforming and by expressing myself without fear of judgment. Every day I'm doing that a little bit more and becoming braver a little bit more each day.

TAYLOR SHINES BRIGHT

Taylor is a student at The Bolles School in Florida and is a member of the Boys and Girls Club of America. She has donated over 5,000 books to her community and spoke at the 2017 March for Science in Washington, D.C. If you'd like to donate to Taylor's GoFundMe to help send girls to see *A Wrinkle in Time*, you can do so here: https://www.gofundme.com/astronaut-starbright-fund. You can also find Taylor on Instagram at @astrostarbright.

Taylor meets Mae Jemison at the Clark Atlanta University commencement 2016. Photo courtesty of the Richardson family.

EAT LIKE AN ASTRONAUT

Did you know there's no gravity in outer space? Because of that, everything floats around, even food! Astronauts eat foods like freeze-dried ice cream and sticky peanut butter. In space, astronauts can't eat bread because crumbs can ruin the spaceship, so they eat tortillas instead. Hungry yet? Make your own space-inspired snack .

TORTILLA MOONS ARE PERFECT FOR A CRUMB-FREE MESS

MAKE ROCKET FRUIT KABOBS USING ALL YOUR FAVORITE FRUIT

CUT CHEESE INTO STAR SHAPES FOR AN EXTRA FUN SNACK

COLOR ME BRAVE

Art from our favorite little people on the planet: you!

Brooklyn, age 7

Maria, age 12

Alya, age 8

Grace, age 9

Sarah, age 8

Luke, age 8

Emily, age 7

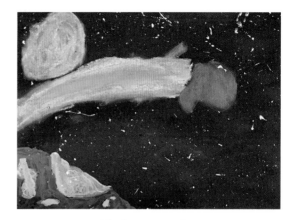

Claire, age 8

Norah, age 9

Adelle, age 6

Faeryn, age 11

Keaton, age 10

Eliza, age 11

Margot, age 8

GALACTIC FACTS

THEY'RE OUT OF THIS WORLD!

1. ASTRONAUTS RETURN TO EARTH **2-3** INCHES TALLER THAN WHEN THEY LEFT.

2. PUTTING ON A SPACESUIT TAKES **45** MINUTES!

3. AN APOLLO ASTRONAUT LOST HIS WEDDING RING DURING HIS TRIP to the MOON AND FOUND it AGAIN DURING A SPACEWALK.

WHEW!

4. ONE MILLION EARTHS COULD FIT INSIDE THE SUN.

hello.

5. ASTRONAUTS USE LIQUID SALT AND PEPPER.

S P

6. SHHH SORRY.

SPACE IS COMPLETELY SILENT.

ILLUSTRATED BY MIKE LOWERY.

TURN AROUND!
BORING STUFF →
BLACK HOLE AHEAD!
WATCH OUT!
PARENT SECTION AHEAD →
FUN STUFF ←

#MOVINGTOSPACE

Do your kids ever make you wish you could move far away? Like, to space? Here are some parents that feel the same way.

@mishay8 That time that my 5 year old made commentary on the shopping habits of the person in front of us at the grocery checkout. "Well that's not healthy. They've got a LOT of chocolate and two tomatoes."

@geeseandganders I was in the garage two weeks ago when I heard my four year old say "I cut my own hair!" And in that frozen moment I muttered "please be talking to your doll"...and she was not. After collecting her beautiful blonde hair...I'm ready to be #movingtospace to recuperate.

@allmom4 My daughter was 4 years old and we were playing outside with our neighbors. Bethany was not being nice to the neighbor kids so I sent her inside to take a break. A few minutes later I allowed her back outside to play. And didn't think much about it. Then, that night as I crawled into bed, hanging on the wall next to my pillow was a note from her: "Mother's Day is cancelled." and a little sad face with tears labeled, "sad mom."

@kiasa Dropping my 6 year old son off at school one morning I cheerfully said, "Know Mom loves you!". Wide-eyed and stone faced he tearfully whispered, "No mom loves me?"

@recipe4cute When my oldest son was about 4 years old, he and 3 other friends snuck off to the bathroom, dumped an entire bottle of baby powder on the tile floor and my friend and I walked in to find them all naked making snow angels.

@melindajoywrites That one time I overheard the kids celebrating the first snow of the year (!!) and then realized that it wasn't snowing outside, it was snowing inside. Powdered sugar. In the dining room. And now I'm #movingtospace. I hear it doesn't snow there.

Submission by Shelley Couvillion

"MY PARENTS WERE THE BEST SCIENTISTS I KNEW BECAUSE THEY WERE ALWAYS ASKING QUESTIONS." –Mae Jemison

WALKING THROUGH FEAR

Essay by Alexandra Elle
Photo by Erika Layne

Transforming fear into curiosity, self-trust, and vulnerability

A part of being human is walking through fear while also attempting to figure out ways to navigate the balance of vulnerability, curiosity, and self-trust. I am a firm believer that we need fear to understand the most profound and intimate parts of ourselves. Not only can it be a catalyst for change, but it can also encourage us to step into our best self. As a mother of an almost 10-year-old, fear knocked me on my back when it clicked that she and the baby I am currently growing would be so far apart in age. I am not sure why it hit me as hard as it did, but I was faced with a lot of seemingly earthshattering questions like, will I remember how to do this? Will my firstborn be okay with the shift of roles going from the only to the oldest? Not only that, I wasn't partnered when I had my daughter. Now that I am married, and we are happy blended family, my fear constantly questions how I will navigate the space of having consistent help and unconditional love from my husband. Not that that's a bad thing by any means, but once you've been superwoman-mom for so long, it can be scary to take off the cape.

With my fear coming to the surface to make its presence known, I could do one of two things. Ignore it and flee like a mad woman. Or root deeply into myself and greet the fear with curiosity. I will be honest, the first option piqued my interest most, but I decided to go with the latter. Attempting to figure out why something frightens us or how to move through our anxieties isn't a simple task. It's a unique challenge for each of us, but in that space of discomfort curiosity lies and waits for its cue to teach.

As parents, addressing our fears, whatever they may look like, requires a certain amount of trust and vulnerability. We often think of those words as exteriors. For example, I need to trust people or I need to be vulnerable with others. However, in reality, turning those two things inward can create a better sense of self-awareness and self-realization. They can create lessons and within those lessons we can take a look at how fear can actually serve versus stifle us. We do our best to teach the children we're rearing how to be brave and resilient by conquering

what scares them, we as parents must do the same. Not only to set a positive example for the youngsters in our lives but also to live in the space of emotional freedom over fearfulness.

In my case, emotional freedom looks like trusting the process and not letting worry be the driver of my life. In order to walk through fear, we have to challenge our way of thinking. Perhaps, even, be motivated and curious by what terrifies us most. Doing that can be

step one in greeting fear head on, and it creates a platform that allows us to be vulnerable with others and ourselves.

Transforming fear into curiosity, self-trust, or vulnerability is daunting but worth the adventure. We can learn so much about ourselves when we address our trepidations head on. In turn, we are able to teach our children how to move through the world in a way that is vibrant, healthy, and meaningful.

MAE WAS CURIOUS AND YOU CAN BE TOO

An exercise about using curiosity to move through fear

Mae is a self-proclaimed scaredy cat, but what's so inspiring about her is the ability she has to let her curiosity take the lead instead of her fear. She never let fear hold her back from what she really wanted to do, and that curiosity resulted in amazing accomplishments. Recognizing our own fears, where they come from, and how to move past them can be a scary and uncomfortable undertaking. What would happen if you allowed your curiosity to lead you through your fears? What would be on the other side? Use these journal questions to reflect.

WHAT SCARES YOU IN LIFE?

IN WHAT WAYS DO YOU THINK YOU CAN MOVE BRAVELY THROUGH FEAR?

HOW ARE YOU TEACHING YOUR CHILDREN RESILIENCE?

WHAT DOES YOUR VULNERABILITY LOOK LIKE TODAY?

"BIG CONVERSATIONS"
Submitted by Jess Racklyeft

A Mom's Guide to SPACE VACATIONS

ENJOY:

Amazing views

Universal childcare

← Black hole

Diaper disposal

Highchair-free brunching

BUT PLEASE EXERCISE CAUTION:

Beware of floating objects

Rips in the space-time continuum

Unfamiliar customs

Hello

A REMINDER:

Visit the nearest mother's room to enjoy the infinite silence of space (and bottomless mimosas).

Mom! Mom my! Waahhh! Mom...

MOTHER'S ROOM

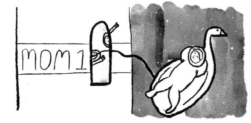

mom 1

CHELSEA

BROUGHT TO YOU BY:

STAFF

Ashley Aikele - Co-Founder, Art Director
Elyse Beard - Co-Founder, Editor-in-Chief

TEAM

Addie Vivas - Wholesale Manager
Alden Aikele - Web Ninja
Dale Beard - Finance Wizard
Kristi Johns - Strategist
Caity Bennett - Consulting Editor

ARTISTS AND ILLUSTRATORS

Alyssa Gonzalez - 11
Andrea Stegmaier - 40
Betsy Petersen - 12
Chelsea Larsson - 63
Emily Kastner - 26, 27, 41, 55
Ilka Mészely - 25, 28
Jacqueline Nguyen - 18
Jacob Souva - 47
Kate Miss - 15, 31, 43
Kristen Solecki - 29
Libby VanderPloeg - 20, 21
Lydia Nichols - 34, 35
Maddy Nye - back cover
Maggie Cole - cover, 6-10, 19, 22-24
Mike Lowery -54
Rocio Ledesma - 13

FIND US HERE

SUBSCRIBE www.braverymag.com
INSTAGRAM @bravery_mag
FACEBOOK Bravery Mag
CONTACT hello@braverymag.com

SPECIAL THANKS TO OUR SPONSOR

GEESE & GANDERS
MODERN MERRIMENTS

PHOTOGRAPHY

AP Photo/Houston Chronicle,
Marie D. De Jesús -38
Bettman/Getty Images -38
Christal Bridge - 30, 36, 37
Erika Lane - 59
Jensen Hande - 48
NASA - endpages, 39
NASA/Roger Ressmeyer/
Corbis/VCG/Getty Images - 5
©Paramount/Courtesy
Everett Collection - 38

SPECIAL THANKS TO

Mardi Fuller
Nasiya Acklen
Alisa Reynolds and the students and faculty of Butte Middle
School in Arco, ID
Ruth O'Loughlin and the students and faculty of Lakeside
Elementary in Lake Village, AR